Ignite Positive Change
for
Generational Success

FERDINAND NDUWINDAVYI

ISBN 979-8-88832-774-6 (paperback)
ISBN 979-8-88832-776-0 (digital)

Christian Faith Publishing
832 Park Avenue
Meadville, PA 16335
www.christianfaithpublishing.com

Printed in the United States of America

Contents

Section 1

Understanding the Future

Chapter 1

Understanding Time

We may know what happened in our past and what we have done right or wrong. We may know what is happening in our present moment. The next minute belongs to the future. How we will live that moment depends on the already known parameters of the past and present. Finally, the future becomes more important than the past and present. It needs to be prepared and planned well. How we will live the next minute or the next century depends on how we live this decisive moment.

We have today the opportunity and possibility to correct, align, restore, and add to what already exists to progress in everything in our life. The future is in our hands today. Your tomorrow might be more significant than today, and the choice must be made now. When we talk about tomorrow, there are four things in mind. The word *tomorrow* speaks about time, but time is now. Tomorrow is a factor of now. There is no tomorrow that stands alone. Whatever you are waiting for tomorrow is waiting for you now. The Bible says in John 4:22,

> Yet a time is coming and has now come when
> the true worshipers will worship the Father in the
> Spirit and in truth, for they are the kind of wor-
> shipers the Father seeks.

The "time is coming" means tomorrow for those waiting for it and implies knowledge. However, the "time is come now" for those who can see it, and the time means revelation, which brings us to say that in the spiritual realm, there is no time notion of yesterday, today, or tomorrow, but time is a revelation. Whenever your eyes open to truth, it brings that truth from the future to the present. The tool to bring that truth from the future to the present is hope. Faith shows us what shall happen in the future, and hope draws the substance we hope for in the present as the scripture says in Hebrews 11:1,

> Now faith is the substance of things hoped for,
> the evidence of things not seen.

Without revelation, it is not easy to understand time. Jesus wept over Jerusalem because the Jews did not have the revelation of the time as is well captured in Luke 19:41–42:

> And when he drew near and saw the city, he
> wept over it, saying, "Would that you, even you,
> had known on this day the things that make for
> peace! But now they are hidden from your eyes."

Tomorrow Means Now

One telephone company advertised its product by saying, "Buy this mobile phone of tomorrow, and tomorrow starts today and now." In the spiritual realm, God is not living in time but in eternity. In Genesis 8:22, God said,

> As long as the earth endures, seedtime and har-
> vest, cold and heat, summer and winter, day and
> night will never cease.

He created things to respect times and seasons. The context means God finishes things before man starts in the spiritual realm.

The prophet Isaiah confirmed this statement in his book in chapter 46 verse 10 where God said,

> I make known the end from the beginning, from ancient times, what is still to come. I say, my purpose will stand, and I will do all I please.

So the time of God is over. He finished creating. He had already assigned a man to what he had already completed. Then when the man realizes his work is finished, he starts his assignment. So we are not waiting for the right time but the true revelation. You can never keep a man who has realized his time in a box. Only the devil holds you until the truth you have sets you free. The length it takes is determined by the time you take to comprehend your revelation. Hence, your "now" is in your revelation. However, the main problem is procrastination. People like to push forward what God wants them to do right now. The scripture says in Hebrews 11:1,

> Now faith is confidence in what we hope for and assurance about what we do not see.

Underline "now." The reality of faith is in the *now* of revelation. Faith never arises before revelation, meaning that faith flows from revelation and is the foundation of faith.

Tomorrow Means Destiny

Tomorrow is the factor of destiny. Whenever God makes a man, the essence is that he has already set his destiny. We are predestinated because our life is set before we are born. Your life is foreknown. Some years ago, the word of the Lord came to Jeremiah, saying,

> Before I formed you in the womb, I knew you, before you were born, I set you apart; I appointed you as a prophet to the nations. (Jeremiah 1:4–5)

It means that there is a "you" that God knew before a "you" that men know. When God says he knows you, it does not mean that men have a cognitive ability to understand you. If I say that I know you, I mean knowing your capacity, totality, and potential. It means knowing what I can do with and through you. It is about knowing your area of gifting where you can be more productive. I know what pressure you can withstand. I know what trials you can carry. I know how much wisdom you have. I know you in your totality. When God knows a man, he knows all things in the man. By the time he releases the man, he has released a creature that will be able to do everything that he has purposed for it to do. If anything happens to you, it is because God knows you. When a person says he knows a car, that does not only mean driving the car. It includes its capacity and functionality. Before he finished you, he did not know you yet. But he knew you after he had completed you. Upon your completion, he put destiny into you. Destiny becomes the drive of the finished man. God begins to push you to your destiny because he has put the capacity in you.

Tomorrow is destiny, and the future is not in front of you. The future is on the inside of you. God does not show you the destination. He puts that place in your spirit. The secret of destiny is that God is already where you are heading. God has invested destiny in you. He is waiting for you at the finish line. The thing about destiny also means that destiny speaks about the prepared stuff. There cannot be destiny without preparation. God prepares before he creates. God set the table before he invites the guests. Either you are going to prepare or you are going to live for the prepared. Destiny is when a man lives for the ready. Destiny is when you find what is yours. God prepared a helper for Adam and brought her to him when he was sleepy. He was surprised, looking at Eve:

> This is now bone of my bones and flesh of my
> flesh; she shall be called "woman," for she was
> taken out of man.

That proves that God never creates before he prepares. Your life is about discovery, not creativity, because nothing is new under the sun as the Scripture says in Ecclesiastes 1:9:

> What has been, will be again, what has been done will be done again; there is nothing new under the sun.

God has created everything, even what the eyes have never seen; the Scripture confirms the paradigm in 1 Corinthians 2:9:

> Eye has not seen, nor ear heard, nor have entered the heart of man. The things which God has prepared for those who love Him.

Then everyone must choose to be in the kitchen or dining table. Tomorrow speaks about a man walking in the prepared things.

Tomorrow Means Vision

You cannot speak about tomorrow unless you have seen it. The power of tomorrow is in today's vision. You will get tomorrow what you have seen today. Tomorrow is not a surprise to a man that can foresee, but tomorrow will be a surprise for a man that cannot have a revelation. Tomorrow is vision. Vision is not what a man sees. It is God's dreams put in the spirit of a man. When God says,

> And it shall come to pass afterward that I will pour out My Spirit on all flesh; Your sons and your daughters shall prophesy, your old men shall dream dreams, your young men shall see visions.

These young men can see visions because God has poured his spirit on all flesh. And after the Spirit has been poured in all flesh, God can ask, "What do you see?" as He asked

> Moreover, the word of the Lord came to me, saying, "Jeremiah, what do you see?" And I said, "I see a branch of an almond tree." Then the Lord said, "You have seen well, for I am ready to perform My word." (Jeremiah 1:11–12)

Vision is an overflow of the Holy Spirit in a man's life. Vision is not your dream because God will not anoint your dreams. He will not sustain what he did not start himself. He is the beginning and the end. Hence, he activates his dreams in you. True vision is not what the man sees but what is revealed for him to see. In Genesis chapter 37:9, the Bible says that Joseph had another dream and told it to his brothers;

> "Listen," he said, "I had another dream, and this time the sun and moon and eleven stars were bowing down to me."

He did not even know that he would be in Pharaoh's court one day. He did not determine what to see in the vision. Abram has his own life in his native country. But the *Lord* told him in Genesis 12:1:

> Go from your country, your people, and your father's household to the land I will show you.

We are not producing the things of God because we are not seeing the things of God. Stop dreaming your dreams and begin to see God's. Tomorrow is a painting that God has already finished waiting for a man to interpret. The purpose of the Holy Spirit is to translate the images of God. Everyone has things he must see and was born to produce. You cannot make what you cannot see, and you cannot see unless the Holy Ghost has revealed it to you. The spirit is the offspring of God. You might start seeing what the Lord wants you to know to be effectively productive.

Tomorrow Means Eternity

Understand that tomorrow never comes. Every tomorrow has its tomorrow. Throughout my country and the countries I visited, I saw adverts on different shops saying, "Debt tomorrow" or "gift tomorrow." That promise is always there whenever you go to the said shops. This is a spiritual mystery because God has created us with eternity in our hearts. That is the reason we are born again. Also, there is no determined day of your blessing. Instead, you receive eternal life of your blessing. God does not say you will be famous for specific years. He gives you eternal life because you are a carrier of eternity. Hence, eternity becomes a mindset of the spiritual man. I do not live for now. I live for eternity. When you understand that, you will not fight with people trying to fight you for a short time while you live in eternity. We carry eternity in us. God anoints and gives you his grace for eternity. He blesses and transforms you eternally. God is not waiting for you to seek him. He has forever revealed himself to you. If you want to see Him, there will never be a day you cannot see God. When you plan to go to the mountains to see God, you will find him because you took him to that place. Eternity means that the anointing does not depend on performance but eternity.

As tomorrow is time, vision, destiny, and eternity, a well-managed mistake today may be an excellent opportunity for destiny. A failure worked on today may constitute the starter of a brilliant success for eternity. A present success should be a tool for more extraordinary achievement rather than a deadlock to the generation's higher development. Today's defeat may become a vision and ingredient or an energizer to become more than a conqueror.

Watching *The Catch* show, I understood a peculiar lesson. A big contender entered the stage accompanied by a beautiful slim lady. They kissed before the match. While the lady stayed outside the ring, the man participated in the fight. It was not an easy fight: He was bruised, kicked, and almost crashed. But at the end of the match, he got the title. What impressed me instead was the attitude of the lady watching like any other fan. She got up, grabbed the fighter's title, and started raising it, shouting, "Yes, we did it" even though she did not lift her tiny finger to help his friend. The fighter was a conqueror, but the lady was more than a conqueror. I understand that it takes someone else to get through the stricter situation for us to celebrate in peace. We do not have enough time to make all our mistakes to get the best future. The suffering of others is a great school to go beyond what they have achieved.

Successful people do not do different things but do them differently. Doing something the same way brings about the same results. I used to tell my younger friends that if they wanted to be better than me, they must perform at least as well as I did in each area I succeeded. In addition, they must correct my mistakes and perform better than me. In that way, none would blame my mistakes as far as they will help shape a better man. Everything that exists is necessary depending on how we use it for the best future. Usually, life lessons are more challenging when your tomorrow is excellent. Every grade level in school has its exams, and we are qualified for the next level after successfully passing the previous level. The more you go to the higher level, the more challenging the exams are. It is the same in life. If we expect a bright future, we should be able to succeed in today's exams, overcome current challenges, and move forward. I like to say, and I will repeat it, "Today's disappointments are appointments of tomorrow's successes."

In my culture, being a man is not connected to sex. Someone is called a man when he has passed through difficult situations and come out alive and a winner. We must be men, not stopped or trapped in despair for our future. Keep moving forward; do not give up, and be resilient. The valiant always moves further than an ordinary man. Success is one step beyond your current position.

Someone said that if people doubt how far you can go, then go farther so that you cannot hear them anymore. Tomorrow is better than today, and tomorrow starts today. You need then to sow now a seed of your future and the one for future generations. When we talk about generations, it implies a family, including a father and children, a community with its leader, or a country/kingdom with its president/king. This book will talk about a King knowing that we are kings and priests as the Bible says in 1 Peter 2:9,

> But you are a chosen people, a royal priesthood,
> a holy nation, God's special possession, that you
> may declare the praises of him who called you
> out of darkness into his marvelous light.

It is also about a family and a generation. It concerns your living and unborn children that constitute the next generations. It helps you prepare, educate, and raise your children and offspring. The message and the truth the book carries are generational because our God is generational. This message concerns the reader and the present and generations to come. This book is about the keys to igniting positive change for generational success.

Section 2

A Generation

Chapter 2

A Generational God

A generation is not a slave to things. Instead, things are slaves to generations. Everyone should ask himself why he was born in this generation and what his impact will be on future generations. The time of your birth determines the things in your life. God prepares a time before he prepares a thing. You do not tell God to do something in your time. Instead, God determined what shall happen every season and what you shall do in your time. Time nor events or circumstances do not bind God. He is transcendent. He is generational, visionary, manager, and eternal.

God Is Generational

Every generation is marked by three things: the word, the spirit, and the manifestation of that generation. Every generation has a predetermined word, and none can possess more than what was saved for his generation. A generation's spirit moves that generation and determines its manifestations.

God Deposits a Word for Every Generation

A word expresses the idea that God wants to manifest in its season. In the New Testament, the Word of God manifested itself in Jesus Christ for the ultimate purpose of saving and redeeming what was lost. The accomplishment of that word produced salvation. We are also born to create, to manifest something, and God has already planned for what everyone must make. God works in times and seasons as well as in plans and purposes. God never creates until there is a purpose behind the creation, and he does not move in the time of what he made. Instead, God is in the future of its creation.

We must understand that every generation has an assignment and is born to fulfill that assignment. For example, the Old Testament must prepare for the coming of Jesus Christ. All the prophecies were about the appearance of the great King Jesus. There is a period when John the Baptist was born between the two testaments. His purpose was to be the forerunner of Jesus Christ. Therefore, it was impossible to get the revelation of the New Testament in the old one. Even the prophets were not to comprehend the true meaning of their prophecies because God had prepared a New Testament's word for the New Testament's generation.

God decides what he deposits. You cannot be any more significant than what he deposited in you. The word of the generation is the seed that starts to grow in that generation to bear everlasting fruit. From the beginning, God has manifested himself as a light producer and creator of everything. What he produced impacted all the generations that came after. He thought about the next generations. We might reproduce what he made using his processes as we are created after his image and likeness. Every season has a vocabulary evolving from the word of the corresponding generation. But that vocabulary must impact the next generations. Then God must first give the word to a generation that will represent him in that generation preparing the next generations to fulfill their assignments.

God Always Puts a Spirit in a Generation

Moses, the friend of God, never prayed in tongues because he was not born in the time of the Holy Spirit. Even though he was speaking face-to-face with God, the latter could not deposit the Holy Ghost in him. The Holy Spirit was reserved for another generation. That is called the generation's spirit. The Scriptures say in Joel 2:27,

> Afterward, the Lord will pour out my Spirit on all people. Your sons and daughters will prophesy, your old men will dream, and your young men will see visions.

There are things prepared for you in this very generation. We are born in the season of prophecy. We do not need to struggle for it. This generation is known for the prophetic utterances that it releases.

There Are Manifestations in Every Generation

For example, those born in the United States of America between 1946 and 1964 were called baby boomers. The manifestation of that season was due to the histrionic upsurge in birth rates after World War II. Armed forces returned home from the war and spent more time with their spouses producing children. It increased the population of the United States. The spirit of a generation has a kind of manifestation that drives it.

God is generational. When God speaks to someone, he honestly talks to his generation and offspring. He told Abraham in Genesis 12:2 that he would be the nation's father. Yet he had no child at that very moment. But God knew that there were generations within Abraham. He blessed Abraham and confirmed that his blessing would affect his offspring and all nations of the earth. The Bible states in Genesis 22:18,

> And in your offspring shall all the nations of the
> world be blessed, because you have obeyed my
> voice.

One generation shall commend his works to another and declare his mighty acts (Psalm 145:4). We also know that his mercy is for those who fear him from generation to generation (Luke 1:50 ESV).

The psalmist acknowledged that God cares about the prayer of the despised, the prisoner, those doomed to death, the widows, and orphans. According to the Scriptures in the book of Psalms 102:18,

> Let this be recorded for the next generation; the
> people yet to be created will praise the Lord.

This incredible act of God endures forever and applies even to those who are yet to be born. God also reigns forever. His kingdom is everlasting, and his love is unending. Daniel proclaimed in his book in chapter 4 verse 3:

> How great are his signs, how mighty his won-
> ders! His kingdom is an everlasting kingdom,
> and his dominion endures from generation to
> generation.

In his essence, God is eternal and has no beginning and no end. He is the source of everything and all law, principles, processes, and statutes. Thus, he remains forever. He has no shadow of change. His precepts have been established for generations. His is generational. A generation goes and a generation comes, but the earth remains forever. Yes, the world and the fullness thereof are God, and his Word stands beyond time and circumstances.

Based on these few statements proving that God is generational, everyone needs to prepare a worthy life for their children. You may be barren or old to pretend to be bearing children. Sara was ninety years old, and by God's power, he delivered a son to Abraham. You should also have grandchildren. You may be godfather or godmother to someone who needs this revelation. Grab advice and apply this message to the next generations. The message especially concerns you who want to see your offspring living well. Please read and understand it, grasp the secret, and apply it immediately.

In the creation process, God spoke to the earth concerning plants. In Genesis 1:11, he said,

> Let the earth bring forth grass, the herb-yielding seed, and the fruit tree-yielding fruit after his kind, whose seed is in itself, upon the earth: and it was so. (KJV)

In the same way, God only created one man putting all the generations into him. Likewise, you have generations in your womb. This message also concerns generations inside you. It would help if you prepared those generations to live well. Our God is generational. And he created us after his image and likeness. That means we have the same generational characteristics and operating systems. Only thinking about yourself means you are killing generations trapped on your inside. Open your mind, and plan for the future of your offspring after your death.

God—The Greatest Visionary

A visionary can be defined as someone with a strong vision of the future. Every human is a visionary because we have the same essence as our Creator. You were created to have a strong vision of your future that God has prepared for you. God is a great visionary. He planned the sky with its clouds, moon, stars, and sun. He envisioned the sea with its white waves, fish, and coral. He expected the giraffe with its giant spots, extra-long eyelashes, and black tongue. And he envisioned you.

The book of Psalm 139:15–16 states,

> Like an open book, you watched me grow from
> conception to birth; all the stages of my life were
> spread out before you, the days of my life all pre-
> pared before I had even lived one day.

Before you took your first breath, God had a strong vision for your future. Every phase of your life was laid out before him before your birthday. He is a visionary, and because His Spirit lives in you, you are also a visionary even when you do not feel like a visionary. Then you need to seek God and ask him to reveal his vision for you. He has projected your relationship with him every moment in all areas of your life. Now it is your turn to switch into visionary mode and get the divine dream about what God has planned for you.

Habakkuk 2:2 says,

> Write the vision; make it plain on tablets, so he
> may run who reads it.

God wants you to take time to understand his vision for your life and operate within its framework. Be ready to receive the reve-lation of God's vision for you and act upon it. Be a person of action and take practical steps until the idea becomes a reality. James 1:22 say, "*Do not merely listen to the word, and so deceive yourselves. Do what it says.*" Write those steps down, read what you wrote, and read it often. Keep it in front of your eyes, and then you can run with it and live the life God has intended for you.

King David told his audience one day that he had never seen the seed of a righteous man begging for bread. When I said our God is generational, I meant he has a vision for those generations. He sees the end from the beginning. I repeat that he testified about himself in the book of prophet Isaiah 46:10 saying,

> He declares the end from the start and from
> ancient times the things that are not yet done.

We are created in visionary God's likeness, and we must be visionary men and women, visionary Christians rather than born-again beggars. Why did King David proclaimed that he never saw a seed of a righteous man begging? Because before God created man, he first prepared everything that man would need including salvation.

God—Manager of Managers

It is not appropriate to compare God with a manager because every attempt at comparison can only describe some aspects. God is called the King of kings, the Lord of lords, and the Lord of Host. I can rightly say that he is the Manager of managers. When he created the earth and its fullness, he put humankind to manage his creation. Moreover, every human race was trapped in the first man Adam. He has made managers, and he remains the manager of managers. Though some people think God looks on this earth from a great distance and that he only influences the lives of very few people willing to be controlled, he remains the author and the finisher of everything and processes all things.

He said,

> For I know the thoughts that I think toward you,
> saith the Lord, thoughts of peace, and not of evil,
> to give you an expected end. (Jeremiah 29:11)

He told Jeremiah he had chosen him from his mother's womb and appointed him to be the prophet to nations. God sees even children yet to be born and has prepared an excellent plan for their life, present, and future. That generational and visionary God also has a plan for those generations. He has thoughts of peace, not evil, to give you a promising future and end. God has a plan of peace for your offspring. What a wonderful God. If we struggle daily, it is not about our God because He has prepared our peaceful future.

When King David said: "I have been young, and now I am old," he meant he observed, monitored, evaluated, controlled, investigated, researched, interviewed people, prayed, and got visions and revelations. He concluded that he had never seen the righteous begging bread. He may have traveled to countries, talked to kings, played music, and fought battles. Even then, he has never seen a righteous man forsaken.

Your neighbor can forsake you. Your pastor can forsake you. Your parents can forsake you. Your spouse can forsake you. Job's wife forsook him, and we are not more special than Job. Everyone you see or meet may forsake you. Even though that situation can happen, God will never forsake you if you are righteous. You can go through the fire, but God will be with you in the fire. He had done it with our fellows Shadrack, Meshack, and Abednego. He will never change as he does not have a shadow of change in his character. You can suffer under heavy rains, but God will be your umbrella. God will do everything under one condition: being righteous. This is the sine qua non condition to prepare an excellent future for your offspring. Be righteous. It is not difficult to be righteous. God said be holy as I am. In other words, be righteous as I am. We know that everything is possible to God. When he asks us to do something, we can easily do it. The reason is that God has already provided everything he needs from us. When God wants us to be righteous, he has already offered righteousness through Jesus Christ.

Chapter 3

A Generational Success

I am proud to be a first-generation in a family to understand that a definite sense of success comes universal and God's principle to carry on a habit. The Bible says in Hebrews 3:4,

> Some man builds every house, but he that built
> all things is God.

Every home has its principles on how to manage its business. Most of those management strategies carry unfailing values leading to generational successes.

With more than fifty years of life, I understood how rare successful generational businesses are based on my family experience and entourage. I never saw a family-owned business survive into the second generation. Let us consider inheritance as a practice of passing on property titles, debts, rights, and obligations upon the death of an individual to an heir. The inheritance guidelines differ between societies and have changed over time but still have played a significant role in human societies. Being a father of five daughters without an heir son as per our tradition, I questioned myself about how to break that failure and start a sustainable success starting from my generation. That needs understanding generational succession, solid principles, and embracing a related paradigm shift. Speaking to followers of my age, most of them are thinking about the family succession of their properties. In some critical cases, conflicts on the issue of succession lead to killing and maiming between family members. It is difficult to realize how fore generations played a part in their decision to stay with the same family business when the number of beneficiaries consistently increases in each new generation.

For my family, I cultivated the mindset by saying that we are stewards of the land for the next generation. My daughters know our wealth belongs to all of us and will not shift to another family. If they decide to marry outside the country, which is their right, their wealth will stay in the family. These are the rules governing the inheritance in my nuclear family. It means that our family is part of something bigger than our generation. I used to tell my daughters that my success in every area of life would be measured by how they will raise their children, my grandchildren. This needs the next generations' determination, enthusiasm, ability, and willingness to perpetuate the incredible opportunity the family provides. Every decision our family makes on our wealth is based on an expectation that our daughters will become second-generation business owners. The Apostle Paul told his son Timothy in his second epistle in chapter 2 verse 2:

> The things that you have heard from me among
> many witnesses, commit these to faithful men
> who will be able to teach others also.

Our goal is to be the parents who have set a solid foundation and can pass on wealth to a second generation more capable than our parents. Every new generation should be more robust and better than the previous. This family commitment would constitute a driver of change, hoping that another generation will follow our paths.

Since my younger age, I did not ever know something my father did that could inspire me in my lifetime. It is sore to say this to a dear one. But that is where I still appreciate my mother after she passed away. My father was intelligent and hardworking, writing in a notebook everything he was doing. I think I have gained that habit. He also traveled to countries to seek jobs, though he did not accomplish anything significant. Instead, I saw my mother build a house in which my dad boldly stayed. May I say that his talents were squandered? I loved him. When he divorced my mother, I stayed with him. I wished I could stay around him. He was still a good dad, and I hoped he could be great until I realized he did not want me to continue the school. That was contrary to mam's wish.

My mother deployed her effort to pay my school fees. Thus, I started to learn from both parents: positive behaviors from my mom and worse things to avoid to live a better life from my dad. I wish he were alive to teach his lessons to you. However, I will share what I learned from his many failures. When you understand "don'ts" from my dad, you will have powerful routines and habits for a well-lived life.

He taught me to work hard and shrewdly. In such a domain, I was the best in my neighborhood. I could work and produce better than all my siblings together. That value is still helping me even in my professional life. I have three colleagues in the office. Two can take their leave simultaneously, but my supervisor would never accept letting me take my leave unless both of my colleagues are present on duty.

Dad used to wake up early irrespective of the weather and worked hard the whole day before he went to snack bars in the evening. I also started working the same way except for drinking alcohol. I was his great companion, hence not good enough for schooling. At an early age, this lifetime message of always being at work was grabbed. I became the courageous boy in my family without the firstborn who got a scholarship abroad. Today, I am used to starting work before sunrise until dusk. For me, work is praise and worship to God. Work is the first assignment God has ever given man.

As said before, dad did not care about my school education. Today, I value my children's education to enable them to receive what I never received from my dad. Even in error, there are things to admire and remember. I also completed my degree in agriculture, a master's degree in leadership and management at United Kingdom Anglia Ruskin University and a doctorate in business administration—International leadership at California Intercontinental University. Presently, I have started several businesses and led some organizations. The rationale is not about my degrees. I intended to testify that the values I received from my parents' controversial characters became my springboard to reaching my current position. If I can do it, you can do it better.

Section 3

Righteousness

Chapter 4

Righteousness—A Key to Generational Success

Righteousness is a theological concept of being justifiable and morally correct. If you are insulting your neighbor, you are not ethically correct. You are missing your target if you are jealous of your prosperous person. If you are cooking stories against your fellow, you are not morally right. You can correct most of what you do: be on time, regularly attend church services, and listen to the Word of God. But when you step out of the church and start insulting partners, you are not morally correct.

Here is the secret if you did not know: whatsoever you do today will impact your children, even those yet to be born of you. If you are jealous, your offspring will be better than you in jealousy. If you can think about killing or destroying the life of someone, that will negatively affect your descendants. For example, Abraham lied, and his son and grandson also lied.

On the other hand, if you are generous, your descendants will be more generous than you. If you bless people today, pray, and support them when they are in need and strengthen them when they are weak, your generosity will positively affect your descendants. They will live in peace and respect. It would be best if you prepared their lives as of today.

David said,

I have never seen a seed of a righteous begging.

Never. If you want your offspring to live well, you only need to be righteous. Hence, stop doing wrong but do well. Otherwise, you will be preparing a slippery ground for your descendants. Instead, bless those who curse you. Everything you do to the person you see is a seed planted for your future generations.

Chapter 5

The Righteous Never Begs Bread

There are many reasons God will never permit the seed of a righteous to beg for bread.

The Ways of the Righteous

> For the Lord knows the way of the righteous: but
> the way of the ungodly shall perish. (Psalms 1:6)

God will never accept the righteous and his seed to hunger. The principle is another fundamental reason for you to be righteous. And this is not difficult. You need to set positive thoughts and ideas on your mind. Your mind is a magnet. If you think of blessings, you will attract blessings. And if you think of problems, you attract situations. You better continually cultivate good thoughts and remain optimistic. We get what we believe. So think positive, and life will automatically become positive for yourself, your neighbors, and future generations.

> The Lord will not suffer the soul of the righteous
> to famish, but he casts away the substance of the
> wicked. (Proverbs 10:3)

God will meet all the needs of a righteous person. If you are rich and righteous, your children will undoubtedly be rich because a child inherits from his father. If a father is a liar or fornicated, his children will perfect that character. Everyone should therefore be righteous.

Righteousness—God's Throne

Psalm 89:14 says,

> Righteousness and justice are the foundation of
> your throne; Mercy and truth go before your face.

One of the foundations of God's throne is righteousness. When we talk about the throne, it is about the headquarters of the kingdom of any kingship. When you lay the foundation of righteousness in your house, God will establish his kingdom in your home. I know we are living in lack because we have preferred accessories to essential principles. Some of us think X or Y will bless us. Yes, God can use them to bless you, but we have a rich God. Instead of fixing eyes on humans and expecting blessings from him, establish righteousness as a lifestyle everywhere you are, and God will establish his throne wherever its foundation is. Therefore, according to his word in Philippians 4:19,

> God shall supply all your need according to his
> riches in glory by Christ Jesus.

He will not only provide what we want but instead everything we need, not according to our requests or demands but according to his riches in grace. Ephesians corroborate this in 3:20:

> Now unto him, that can do exceedingly abun-
> dantly above all that we ask or think, according
> to the power that worketh in us.

If you ask me, I may not give you because I also have needs and obligations. But this rich Father, our heavenly Father, will provide what you need and even above what you ask or think according to his unsearchable grace. So if you connect to this God who establishes his throne on the foundation of righteousness in your home, your children will indeed lack nothing and will never be forsaken or beg for bread. There is no way your offspring may beg if you have abundance in your home.

The revealed secret here is this: *whatsoever you do today will positively or negatively affect your descendants.* The good news is that it is never late to reconnect, readjust, and prepare for a great future as per the will and plans of our God (Jeremiah 29:11). Only this one remains: become righteous.

The book of Romans 5:12 tells us,

> Wherefore, as by one man sin entered into the
> world, and death by sin; and so, death passed
> upon all men, for that all have sinned.

We understand that by the sin of one man, sin entered the world and has affected all humans. This proves that we were in the womb of Adam. When he sinned, all those who came after him, including you and me, were generations after generations. We were counted as sinners until Romans 5:19 which says,

> For as by one man's disobedience many were
> made sinners, so by the obedience of one shall
> many be made righteous.

The same principle applies to one righteous man. Many were counted as righteous.

Those who seek the righteousness of God will not want.

> O fear the Lord, ye his saints: for there is no want
> to them that fear him. (Psalms 34:9)

What a great strategy to own everything you need only because you fear God and seek his righteousness. That is worth trying. Let us start now. Let us be the doers of the word and not hearers only, deceiving ourselves (James 1:22).

Chapter 6

The Righteous Is Never Forsaken

When I was six, my elder brother was involved in illegal trading. The company he worked for filed a complaint against him, and the police issued an arrest warrant to capture and bring him to justice. That day, I was at home guarding the house as every child used to do in our culture. Suddenly, armed military men erupted at home and threatened to kill me if I did not show where the illicit products were hidden or where my brother was. I responded that I could show them where illegal merchandise was if they allowed me to open the door. They believed even though I sorted a way to run and warn my brother.

At the time, my family members were invited to a party in a neighborhood. I took the opportunity to go through the behind door and run to advise him about the situation. He immediately escaped. My father was present at the feast. You may know that every child thinks his father is a hero. So was I. However, instead of protecting me, he asked me to return home to guard the house as if nothing had happened. He also took the opportunity to escape. At that time, the military men realized I was not home and began searching me around. I was naïve, believing in my father's statement. Hence, the military men arrested me and accused me of complicity in illicit trading. I was brought to the commander who stayed behind when his troops searched our house and the surroundings.

Because of my age, the commander ordered his troops to release me. He cautioned me that I must tell the truth if they came back. I can confess that I was lucky that day. From that situation, I realized that my father was neither a hero nor my protector. Confidence in him was reduced. Later, I understood why my mother was raising us alone, and my father was there contributing for nothing. I grew up believing I would fail until I received Jesus Christ as my Savior and Lord. From there, I understood that even though my biological father forsook me, my heavenly Father will never forsake me. My spouse, friends, brethren, and pastor can forsake me, but God will never forsake me. We know that God uses humans to fulfill his purpose in our lives though they can forsake you.

When I was at college, my schoolmate had a similar last name with a correct and just man who had faithfully served the country. Authorities thought my schoolmate was his real son. Because of that, he was offered—I would say mistakenly—a scholarship to France. He benefited from the righteousness of a person he never knew. The righteous man is never forgotten or forsaken. If political authority can reward the so-called child of a mere man, how much more can our God do to his beloved? The offspring of a mere man was remembered due to his justice. How much more can God remember our descendants if we remain righteous? Indeed, the righteous man is never forsaken.

Section 4

Attitude

Chapter 7

Attitude Determines Altitude

Going through life flying high or just crawling along is determined more by your attitude than anything else. I think that many people do not understand such a principle. Years ago, Zig Ziglar declared, "It is your attitude, more than your aptitude, which will determine your altitude." Attitude refers to your thinking and outlook toward life. Some people are pessimistic, seeing problems at every opportunity. When they fail at tasks, they lose hope and give up. At the same time, others are optimistic and see opportunity in every challenge. They do not give up easily. To succeed in life, you need to be determined to reach your goals, despite the setbacks you face along the way. Skills and knowledge are essential, but they can be acquired with time.

Nonetheless, attitude is inherent in an individual that is difficult to change with time. So if a person is hardworking and keen to succeed in life, he will undoubtedly enhance his skills to climb higher, which is why attitude is considered more important than aptitude. On the other hand, an intelligent yet lazy individual cannot succeed because he lacks the motivation and determination to excel.

How we feel about our experiences in life can either stop us in our tracks or inspire us to action. With the right attitude, human beings can move mountains. With the wrong attitude, they can be crushed by the smallest of grains. Therefore, doing the necessary work to make amends with your past is imperative. No matter how bad it hurt, how angry it made you, or how much of a failure you felt you were, we all have the same two choices: you can let the past overwhelm you, or you can let the past educate you. In choosing the latter, we can bring new wisdom into our everyday experiences and move forward toward a brighter future.

Live Example

Nothing can stop a person with the right mental attitude from achieving his goal. Nothing on earth can help a person with the wrong mental attitude. Life often presents unforeseen curves in the road that can throw us off course. Having a positive attitude is the only sane approach to take. It is essential in the trials and seasons of difficulty that we hold to the path God has placed us on. Trusting God's process will renew and strengthen you to face the journey ahead. Everyone who walks with the Lord experiences the same kind of process.

While there have been seasons in my life filled with an apparent victory over major sin, a little suffering, and unhindered communion with God, there have also been seasons filled with defeat, loss, affliction, and silence. In those moments, I feel tempted to "tank."

Nevertheless, I am reminded by God's word that this is all part of a process: shaping our character. God is now transforming me into the image of Jesus after redeeming me from the grave. God cares more about becoming than reaching, the journey rather than the destination, the process rather than the product.

November 2018 has been a great month in my life. That Sunday, I was in the church with the nostalgia for great brethren I did not see for a while. Instead, I surprisingly learned that I was suspended from ministry in the church, and my brethren have no right to contact me. The unique reason was immoral act. I was quarantined.

You do not know what you can do and accomplish without trying first. So it makes much more sense to adopt a positive attitude toward life and work than defaulting to a negative perspective. I remember 2015—the dangerous year of Ebola in west Africa. Suspected subjects were quarantined to avoid propagation of the virus. Even family members were not authorized to be in contact with their beloved in case of suspected Ebola infection. That was my situation: as if I had a contagious illness.

Your attitude is your choice. This was my saddest day ever. I received a letter of suspension and went home humiliated in front of the whole world, my family, and the entire congregation. The situation was as complicated as I was the church overseer. No one can give you a bad attitude nor can you provide a positive one except *you*. You get to choose. You can think, *I can't stand this awful rainy weather*, or *Guess just what we need—a nice bit of rain to freshen things up*.

Chapter 8

Overcoming Failure

I was inspired by the following words: "If you cannot fly, run. If you cannot run, walk. If you cannot walk, crawl. But, by all means, keep moving." If the right arm cannot throw the ball, try the left arm. Life is about trial and error. Through our failures, we succeed.

If you are talented, you may have difficulty staying positive and teachable. You may act like you know it all. Consequently, it will be difficult for you to keep on growing. In my case, the first reaction was to write back, trying to raise my legal rights to respond and appeal. That was a mere flesh fight. But tough seasons lead to the inner conversations in the locker room of my heart about God's purpose in this loss. I like to define attitude as the orientation of one's mind toward people, things, or situations, particularly under pressure that threatens our "true north."

When times are tough and things are not going our way, we find it difficult to trust God. We doubt that God will come through for us; we lack faith in his promises, and we worry ourselves with endless thoughts about our future. However, God wants us to trust him when we have doubts and are unsure what to do. He wants us to believe in his promises when we think things will get worse.

When I question whether God is working in me for his good pleasure, the Bible reminds me that I can trust the process of sanctification because *the God of peace will himself sanctify me completely"* (1 Thessalonians 5:23) The Lord began this cleansing process when my heart was made alive to him "*will bring it to completion at the day of Jesus Christ*" (Philippians 1:6). He will not leave his new creatures unfinished. So if I press on in the war with my sin, continuing in faith and repentance, trusting the process means that in both my best efforts and my worst failures in working out my salvation, I can be assured that it is God who works in me both to will and to work for his good pleasure.

That led me to the second option to picture, ponder, and evaluate the impact of any action I take. I spent a whole night in prayer to seek God's direction. He told me, "Your attitude would determine your altitude." Beautiful diamonds and the pencil have the same root element: carbon. In the case of diamonds, the atoms are more tightly arranged than in pencil. It is the tightness of the bond that enables their beauty.

Forming bonds that are tight enough to transform carbon into a beautiful diamond requires two things: scorching temperatures and extremely high pressure. The "suffering" the elements go through is what creates their beauty. This process usually occurs in the earth's deep places where naturally elevated temperatures and high pressure exist. When I understood the principle, it was like a black veil was removed from my eyesight. I decided to take this advantage to get shaped by my manufacturer.

I remembered another event that happened more than twenty years before when God sent messengers to tell me that he had put two options in front of me: easy and prosperous life without him or benefit from his presence subject to accepting being bonded on the fire furnace to shape my character for his business and glory. I remembered I chose the second option that time. Hence, I realized that what happened to me was part of his work on me, and I surrendered and spoke out alone saying, "I was ready, God. You promised to stay with me even in the fire. I am ready now." This is what I call an attitude of resilience. Resilience means how quickly you bounce back after a setback. A lack of self-belief and confidence can "keep good people down." A good attitude will allow confronted persons to "dig deep" and to look for the positive and the opportunity rather than dwell on the negative and the threat.

Shortly after my decision, God started sending messengers to me. The first one, a dear pastor from Cameroon, wrote me a message worth being quoted:

> Hello, dear Bishop. May the Holy Spirit sustain you during this hardship period. Please remember that you uplifted and blessed many Christians in the body of Christ. Many are watching to see you how you cross this dam of trials today. I pray you to adopt Jesus's attitude who was accused, tortured, and mocked, but He did not voice a single word. Adopt the Master's attitude and not allow any contrary pressure to quench your spirit. Jesus loves you. We do love you. Your soul and input to build the church are still essential. I plead with tears kneeling before you, begging you deep from the bottom of my heart: remember our Master Jesus's attitude and follow his example. This is the appointed time ever for you to resemble him.

My response was very straightforward. I said, "Indeed, my attitude will determine my altitude. After the night vigil I did, God gave a clear direction on what to do. The great thing is that my heart was ready to submit to the will of God even though his ways were far different from human ways."

God sent a second messenger to my residence the morning after my night prayer. She told me God showed her my situation. He sent her to remember me of all personal promises and covenants of God and take the right attitude. She said, "When the same situation happened to King David, the whole of Israel knew, even the world, including us. *God directed and inspired writers to include the incident in the Holy Bible to teach those who experienced the same circumstances. God loves you.*" I was convinced that God wanted me to take the attitude of Jesus by giving me a living example of David. At that moment, I fell face-first against the ground and started crying for forgiveness. The messenger prayed for me. I felt peaceful and ready to accomplish God's will.

The following day, another messenger came in and told the same message. He said I should adopt the attitude of Jesus and never try to explain myself but should repent. I answered that my mood would determine my altitude but now with more confidence. I was at peace. God has forgiven me, and I was ready for any consequences of my sins.

I met the church board of ethics and discipline on the fifth day and repented. I also had to repent in front of my wife. On the following Sunday, I confessed my sins publicly. I applied the scriptures that ask us to humiliate ourselves under God's mighty hand, and he will elevate us at the appointed time (1 Peter 5:6).

While some fellow brothers in Christ rejoiced in my humiliation, sharing the bad news to the whole world and praising God for permitting Satan to destroy me, others were in sorrow. This is the paradox of a human being. Messages of encouragement and congratulations came from all parts of the world. My boldness to confess my sins publicly bore many fruits. Some of them are worth to be shared.

From Burundi, PB said,

> Shalom brother. I heard of the storm around your home and church. My spouse insisted I call you for comfort, but I would not listen to her. I assure her I know pastor Ferdinand to be a powerful man. He can face whatever storm comes his way. Besides, Ferdinand must be facing a lot by now. Please tell me I was not wrong. Please tell me you are holding on! After all, I was told yesterday that you came out of the trial triumphantly. All of us can fall, but only heroes can stand up again and continue the fight for faith. I trusted you, and I still do. Keep the faith. You are God's child.

My response was precise, concise, summarized, and straight to the point: "Shalom, brother. You were not wrong. I was firm in Jesus.

Also, we are more than conquerors through Him. To be lifted, we must humble ourselves before we are humiliated. However, the result is the same: depending on our attitude, we become the greatest or the wretch."

From Denmark, AN said,

> Dear pastor and brother, receive my greetings. Dear pastor and brother, I sent this message to encourage you and congratulate you for the greatness and dignity you have just shown. The man's greatness is not measured by the number of times he has fallen or by never losing. Instead, it is about falling and getting back up, bouncing around, and continuing the journey—with much respect.

From Middle East GN Afghanistan,

> Dear pastor and friend, I salute you. You are a hero. I heard how you behave in your troubled situation, confessing your sins publicly and asking for forgiveness. Bravo! After such a situation, you are empowered to accomplish great things. I hope others see you as a role model. Satan could rejoice about your achievement and had to attack you. Fortunately, you are more than a conqueror. You are a remarkable man of God and a strong character. Thank God for his grace entrusted to you. You are like the King David of the Bible—a living best example of an effective leader. Keep it up.

The lesson holds for everyone: the difficult things in our lives that we think are obstacles to growth are the very experiences God uses to strengthen us, to refine us, purify us, mold us, and fashion us into the image of his Son. It is a bitter pill to swallow, but daily life's crucible is the furnace of transformation. The famine would have killed Egyptians and Israelites if Joseph had not been put in the pit, sold as an enslaved person, put unjustly in prison to get the opportunity to explain the Pharaoh's dream, and then become the prime minister in a foreign country. David would not have become a famous king after God's heart without the Goliath in his life.

Section 5

Honor

Chapter 9

Faithfully Serve God

Whoever serves me must follow me; my servant will also be where I am. My Father will honor the one who suits me.

—John 12:26

Sources and Kinds of Honor

There are many kinds of honor flowing from different sources. Those who can give honor are also multiple. Honor can stream from your official position, or friends, from great names or history of their parents, the location of your home; those living in the higher standard quarter are more considered than those staying in rural or remote areas. Those who drive expensive cars are more respected than those in old ones; the kind of clothes you wear is also a factor of honor and the size of the body to some extent. All those kinds of honor are temporary but based on righteousness in serving the Lord—the reward you received from the Master of the business who promised to honor those who faithfully serve him. This kind of honor is everlasting.

When God asks you to be righteous, his original intention is for you to be honorable, a person of value. Everyone has access to the position of honor only if he stays righteous. According to the Bible, the sine qua non condition to have incorruptible honor is following

51

Jesus, being where he is, and faithfully serving him; his Father, our Father, will honor him.

During the time of Jesus, the Greeks went to Jerusalem to see and acquire his wisdom. They had the golden principle that a wise is sharpened by another.

> As iron sharpens iron, one person sharpens another. (Proverbs 27:17)

They thought they needed more wisdom to be knowledgeable and renown. They have had that Jesus grew up appreciated by God and men. However, Jesus told them that the authentic way to get honor is through following him and staying with him. If you serve Jesus, God will honor you.

To work together, you need to agree (Amos 3:3). Following him is to agree on the same vision, mind, and result. Staying with him is using the same processes in the same conditions (example of Moses who beat the rock instead of speaking to it).

The first step in serving Jesus is to agree with him. The question is, What can we do to perform the work of God? The work of God is believing in him that was sent (John 6:27–28). Accepting Jesus is the first step to agreeing to work together.

The second step is to follow him. Following him is a threefold principle. First, following Jesus entails having total obedience. This means that you commit to accepting and applying orders from him. When you agree with your employer, you must accomplish any activities in the job description. Jesus is also a good employer. If he tells you to sit, you must sit. If he tells you to pray, you must pray. If he orders you to forgive, you must forgive, and if he tells you to repent, you should repent. Hence, do not despise anyone, but even though you can hate him, the Father in heaven will honor him. You would better honor him who is honored by the father. The first condition to inherit this honor is to have obedience that will lead you to righteousness.

Secondly, following Jesus is to have the same character: *speak like him, act like him, walk like him and think like him.*

> When he found him, he brought him to Antioch.
> So, for a whole year, Barnabas and Saul met with
> the church and instructed many people. The
> disciples were called Christians first at Antioch.
> (Acts 11:26)

People should confound you with Jesus as they did with his disciples. How we would be is not yet revealed, but at that time, we will be like him (1 John 3:2).

Obedience is the key to righteousness and honor.

> But Samuel replied: "Does the Lord delight in
> burnt offerings and sacrifices as much as in obey-
> ing the Lord? To obey is better than sacrifice,
> and to heed is better than the fat of rams. For
> rebellion is like the sin of divination, and arro-
> gance is like the evil of idolatry. Because you have
> rejected the word of the Lord, he has rejected you
> as king." (1 Samuel 15:22–23)

Thirdly, following him is to accept to go through the same trials, dangers, snares, and toils. To be everywhere he is even in trials. This is shown when your friend is in trouble or if you love someone. When you believe someone or in someone, you do not abandon him in the days of crisis; instead, you adamantly support him. Proverbs 17:17 says,

> A friend loves at all times, and a brother is born
> for a time of adversity.

James 1:12 asserted,

> Blessed is the one who perseveres under trial
> because, having stood the test, that person will
> receive the crown of life that the Lord has prom-
> ised to those who love him.

You accept to share with Jesus excellent and bad moments. That is another side of righteousness: remaining faithful at any time.

God promised Joseph that he would be the leader of his family. Based on his brothers' jealousy, he was thrown into the pit. However, Joseph continues to see God's honor even in the hole. When he was sold as an enslaved person, he kept righteousness. When he was wrongly accused and put into jail, he kept his character until he reached the appointed time of his God's promise: the prime minister of a foreign country. Righteousness protected God's promises to him and his family. We go through circumstances and events that we cannot remove the honor God had entrusted us with if we keep righteousness. This righteousness was strengthened by Joseph's obedience toward the heavenly Father who is the dispenser or the provider of honor and righteousness. God gave Joseph honor through obedience in everything he did—as an enslaved person, a prisoner, and a prime minister. God honored him. When you face trials, keep the faith as your attitude determines the honor in the difficult moment.

You are honored and called a hero when you can overcome those difficult situations and come out triumphantly. Some of us die during snares, like some Israelites, due to a lack of faith. But if you can overcome the dangers, you receive blessings and victory prizes. Trials and faith-trying righteousness are the means to win. And then Jesus said, the one whose serves must follow me and stay with me in every situation. Such a person who serves me faithfully and in righteousness will be honored by my father.

In John 20:17 Jesus said,

> Do not hold on to me, for I have not yet ascended
> to the Father. Go instead to my brothers and tell
> them, "I am ascending to my Father and your
> Father, to my God and your God."

When Jesus rose, Mary thought he was a gardener. When he reveals himself to Mary, she wants to hug him emotionally. However, Jesus refused but pronounced a remarkable statement: Go and tell other disciples. I am going to my Father who is your Father, to my God who is your God. This God, his God, and our Lord Jesus Christ's Father will honor you if you serve him. For Jesus, we are no more strangers but friends, brothers, and coheirs.

> Whatever you do, work at it with all your heart,
> as working for the Lord, not for human masters.
> (Colossians 3:23)

Let us do everything we do as those serving our Great Master, not men, the Father of our Lord Jesus, who is also our Father; he can honor us and make us honorable. Henceforth, even your enemies will testify that you are righteous having in the living God in you, and people will respect you and will honor you.

In our local church, a woman called "Cherie" is translated as "Dear." She is not only Cherie to her husband or only in her church but also her professional life. Her employer and colleagues know that she is committed to supporting pregnant women who are about to deliver irrespective of where they belong. She faithfully serves the Lord in church and among non-Christians until everyone calls her Cherie. God has honored her. She received special permission to help her continue serving God faithfully. She maintained her righteous attitude and did not abuse the confidence people had entrusted her.

Righteousness, truth, and faith are the critical components of honorable persons. This is the honor we receive only and only from God.

Chapter 10

Doing Good with Patience

To those who by persistence in doing good seek glory, honor, and immortality, he will give eternal life. But for those who are self-seeking, reject the truth, and follow evil, there will be wrath and anger.

—Romans 2:7–8

Righteousness gives value to your life. Albeit God has prepared great things for us, we miss our divine portion because of ignorance. We focus on accessories instead of essential items. God created everything good and easy, but men searched for his own.

A blind man sat beside the road with an inscription: "Help me because I am blind and miserable." Nevertheless, people did not care about him. A passerby saw the desperate message and understood that the problems of the blind do not preoccupy people because they also have theirs. The person took the inscription and changed the message. He said: "I thank God you see beautiful things that constitute his wonderful creation. If I had eyes to see them, I could praise him tremendously." This message touched everyone. To see a blind praising God when those who can see are preoccupied with things of this world. Also, people started giving him as a sign of praise and remembrance of what God had done for them.

If you want beauty, honor, and eternal life, dwell in doing good with patience. There are many challenges and trials in generosity.

However, it positively impacts the family, person, and even nations. Consequences are also the same for your descendants if you do wrong.

> If anyone, then, knows the good they ought to do and does not do it, it is a sin for them. (James 4:17)

> For we must all appear before the judgment seat of Christ; that everyone may receive the things done in his body, according to that he hath done, whether it be good or bad. (2 Corinthians 5:10)

> But glory, honor, and peace for everyone who does good: first for the Jew, then for the Gentile. (Romans 2:10)

If you do good to someone, you will both be happy. Beyond this happiness, you become honorable. Decide to do good consistently.

If you want your descendants to live in abundance, continue to do good with patience. But if you choose to do wrong, it will also be after the next generation. A righteous man continues to do good for himself (honor) and his offspring. Doing good with patience is a character of a righteous man.

Chapter 11

Integrity

Just as things are getting better for Joseph because his many natural talents are coming to fruition, he is tempted by Potiphar's wife to engage in sexual activity.

Many leaders have enough talent to take them further than their character can sustain them. They shoot up like a rocket and fall like a rock.

Each test of integrity on your leadership journey matters a lot. Temptations of every kind will forge habits that enable you to exercise integrity in the moment of choice, or they will put you on the slippery slope of moral failure. Difficulties of every kind will forge habits that enable you to exercise integrity in the moment of choice.

Joseph resisted the advances from Potiphar's wife. This gave honor to his boss, gave honor to God, but more importantly, and unbeknownst to Joseph, it brought honor and respect to himself.

The integrity lesson can be summarized thus: leading self always precedes leading others. First Samuel 9:6 suggested,

> And he said unto him, behold now, there is in this city a man of God, and he is an honorable man; all that he saith cometh surely to pass: now let us go thither; peradventure he can shew us our way that we should go.

It is possible when someone looks at you and may not call you honorable because his physical eyes do not see God's divine reality and plan for your life. Even though none can call you honorable, you know yourself and should call yourself honorable because of what God has done for you.

A particular Saul, son of Kish, had a donkey. One day, those donkeys were lost, and his father told him to go with a servant to search for them. They searched everywhere unsuccessfully, and Saul told his servant they might abandon and return home so that his father could not wonder about both donkeys and his son. But the servant responded with a high revelation. He agreed that it is true they may go back and added that they should first consult an honorable man of God living in the city in which they were searching. He said it does not cost anything much. The man was, first, a man of God; second, he was honorable, and every declaration he made always happens.

Remember that Jesus said in John 6:29 that the work of God is the belief in the One he sent; you become a servant of God or a man of God. In this town, there is a servant of God. Jesus said he who serves me, my Father will honor him. And in this town, there is an honorable man of God. Every word spoken by him always happens. This is integrity. I define integrity as acting according to someone's word: do what you say and say what you do. Integrity is another component of righteousness. It is impossible to be a righteous person if you can act differently from what you say or if you can say things you cannot do. Many of us have promised things but failed to fulfill our promises. That is the question.

> Samuel grew, and the Lord was with him, and let
> none of his words fall to the ground. (2 Samuel
> 3:19)

Very importantly, God did no more permit Samuel to pronounce something he could not fulfill, and consequently, every word from his mouth was manifested into a reality. Hence for the next generation, let us speak about what we can do. An honorable person fulfills his promises. Some people call that a gentleman's law; I would call it a righteousness principle as written in Mathew 5:37:

> But let your communication be, Yea, yea; Nay, nay: for whatsoever is more than this cometh of evil.

Integrity is to know the required and positive values and act and behave accordingly. It means to act according to your word and speak as your act. We cannot confound reputation and integrity. Reputation is being known for great things, good or bad, you have done. Reputation is the image or the shadow of what you are. It does not express the whole reality. The shadow can be short or extended according to the position of the light source. It also depends on the positive state of mind of the observer. Hence, we know there are renowned people in the world who are unreliable. They have a reputation, but their lifestyle, character, and attitude do not show integrity. They take advantage of their reputation based on those who appreciate them, not on positive values and principles.

The more you match your moral values and actions, the more integrity increases. And the more your integrity increases, the more your honor increases. The values of the honorable man of God matched with what he was saying and doing until people knew there was an honorable man of God in the town. The question is, How do people know you in your city?

One of my values is being on time everywhere and in everything. Then your integrity increases according to how you behave in every situation, and proportionally, it brings about your honor. If you want to be honorable, do not seek to be known but cultivate your integrity.

> If a man vows a vow unto the Lord or swears an oath to bind his soul with a bond; he shall not break his word, he shall do according to all that proceeded out of his mouth. (Numbers 30:2)

Nowadays, if you have an appointment with someone and he is late, you try to inquire about his position. Even a Christian might tell you that he is near and about to arrive. He will avoid telling you the truth to keep you waiting some additional minutes. You asked him about his exact position, but his response is about his commitment to come, which does not answer the question. You recognize a friend driving in front of you and want to greet him. You call him back and express your willingness to greet him physically. When you try to ask about his position, he will tell you he is in a different city. And when you reveal to him that you are behind him, he will cook out another story. But the Bible says,

> Lord, who shall abide in thy tabernacle? Who shall dwell in thy holy hill? He that walketh uprightly, worketh righteousness, and speaketh the truth in his heart. (Psalm 15:1–2)

Let us walk upright, work righteousness, and speak the truth in our heart as we know the mouth speaks the abundance of our heart. To have integrity, our walk, work, and word must match. These are the pillars of righteousness. And we know that a righteous man will never be forsaken or his seeds beg bread.

Unfortunately, people do not walk their talk. Even the Bible provided an example of such people: Ananias and Sapphire (Acts 5:1–10). They had a property and sold it to share with other Christians. But they agreed not to tell the truth about the price they had received on the sale. This lack of integrity cost their lives. It is not men that you lie but the heavenly God. We must walk and work on our talk.

On the other hand, people know the values and what they must do, but they do and say what is far different from the truth. This is the political syndrome. I know what is worth, proper, and correct, but I cannot say or do it because of my position. But I will only say what people want to hear may be to galvanize the electorate and gain or stay in the office. You promise things to the population entirely knowing that you will not be able to accomplish them after you are elected. This political syndrome has also entered the church.

Preachers no longer share the biblical truth by preaching about what church members want to hear so that they can increase their financial income or be appreciated by followers. The Bible says in 2 Timothy 4:3,

> For the time will come when people will not put up with sound doctrine. Instead, to suit their desires, they will gather around them many teachers to say what their itching ears want to hear.

Therefore, righteous men must learn and understand the biblical truth to not fall into the enemy's snare or be blown by any winds. Integrity as a Christian is to apply God's values in our lives and share them with our fellowmen or neighbors.

Section 6

Stewardship

Chapter 12

Principle 322

Principle 322 is a fundamental principle that makes understanding what God means by ideal love possible. This is what I call a perfect management principle. This was a spiritual revelation that I had in reading Mathew 22:37–39:

> Jesus replied, "You must love the Lord your God with all your heart, with all your soul, and with all your intellect." This is the largest and most important command. And here is the second commandment, which is of equal importance: "You must love thy neighbor as yourself."

In the passage that concerns us, we can see three maxims on which we will base our reasoning. There is first the love of God then the love of yourself and finally the love of the neighbor. The two commandments are of equal importance. This means that nothing is to be neglected, and nothing is to be underestimated because the three truths are of equal importance. The three maxims are the most significant in value, meanings, results, and all fields because all the laws of Moses and the teachings of the prophets depend on these three maxims. It also requires the most significant commitment of everyone, let us say your most extraordinary commitment, to achieve the result envisaged by the author of the principle. The revelation that emerges from these maxims is what I call principle 322.

God so loved the world that he gave his beloved son so that whoever believes in him should not perish but that he has the eternal coming. His son did not come to the world to condemn it but to be saved by him. I will say here that the human being is not an enemy of God but a collaborator. God fulfilled all these beautiful plans through man. All essential here is to love God because he loved us first. He loved us when we were still sinners. He loved us when we were still strangers. He loved us before we even knew him. Therefore, to be loved by God is not conditioned by our actions, position, knowledge of scriptures, or zeal in religion or denomination. The love of God is unconditional. We should love him unconditionally. It is instead a path with one direction but with two opposite senses. God loves man, and he wants us to be like him.

For this reason, the author of this passage exhorts us to love God with all our heart, intelligence, and strength. Nothing is greater than the love of God. Nothing can be greater than the love we have for God.

Therefore, we cannot say we love God if we do not like his best friends. Your friend's friend is a friend. He does not necessarily have to be your friend, but he is a friend anyway for the respect of your friend. The quality and quantity of love you love God is proportional to the quality and amount of passion you love men. You cannot say you love God and wish evil to his best creature. You cannot tell yourself to love God if you plan to eliminate people with different opinions. God did not create men with the same thoughts, beliefs, behaviors, and eating habits. He only made man in his image and likeness. He made them with different traits through the richness of his love, so they constituted divine harmony. Two are better than one. Yes, because they complement each other. What is not accessible for one can be for the other. That is why we must always work together with others because we get rich. So why should someone kill another for different opinions? Why does someone entertain the so-called holy war and falsely fight for the God who loves humans? Why then kill in the name of this unfathomable God of love?

Chapter 13

The Measurement of Self

We said this: in the way God has loved us, we must worship him in return. To adore him, he will have to love the man, the neighbor, he created in his image and likeness and whom he loves unconditionally. The closest is yourself. So you cannot say that you love God without loving your nearest citizen. You cannot love your neighbor if you do not love yourself. The prerequisite to saying you love God is the two principles: loving yourself and loving your neighbor. Yes, the love of your God is directly proportional and equivalent to that of yourself and your neighbor.

To love God is to love your neighbor and to love your neighbor means to worship your God. Here is the recommendation: Love God with all your heart, with all your strength, and all your intelligence. To solve this system of equations of the first degree of three equations with three unknowns, we will need a unit of measure: the love that you love yourself.

You may reason that all people at least love themselves. I would answer that this is not as apparent as you think. Everyone knows that smoking is terrible for health including those who smoke. So let us take a soldier on a peace mission in a foreign country. He is always ready to fight the enemy who would come from the outside to maintain that peace. He is prepared to die anytime rather than let the enemy invade and defeat him. This military guy smokes two packs of cigarettes daily to keep his spirits up. Tell me then, you who are more enlightened, how you can accept everything and risking your life so that an external enemy cannot manage to control the territory under your command. Still, on the contrary, you pay an enemy of your health that I call "nicotine" in your own house! How long will you resist the outside enemy if the other one inside has properly done the work he was paid to accomplish: inoculate lung cancer or throat, and I pass. Let us summarize. This military loves the country where he went to maintain peace. But he uses his ballast salary to pay someone who would help him to be eliminated gently. Such a military loves others, but he fiercely hates himself.

Let us analyze this truth by one of the biblical principles: do unto others what you would like them to do to you. What is true for an elephant is also true for an ant. In mathematics, only one counter-example is enough to prove whether the thesis is verified or not. The saying that there is no rule without exception, I would also say that the exception confirms the rule. Let us see what that means.

A friend told me that since over forty years of inter-ethnic conflicts in his country, he has never nurtured any feelings of hatred toward other people irrespective of age, gender, ethnicity, religion, political affiliation, and region. He recently told me he hates people who do not believe that Jesus is God. That was an excellent opportunity to explain that these people with different beliefs are human beings created in the image and likeness of God. The fact that God created them is proof that he loves them. So no one has the right to hate what God has loved and pretend to love God in return.

Chapter 14

Numbers and Stewardship

Loving Your Neighbor

Suppose, for example, that you love yourself about ten liters or five meters or even at seventy kilograms. I do not know what measure to use to express the quantity and quality of love. I want to say that you must love your neighbor with the same amount/quality of love that you love yourself. So you are the unit of measure.

Meaning of Numbers 7, 3, and 2

Imagine a world without numbers. There would be no money. Trade is renumeration to barter. What about sports? Not only would we be unable to count the points, but we could not even determine the number of players to compose a team! Besides that, there are good days; the numbers convey an aura of mystery. It is because they are abstract. You cannot see them, touch them, or feel them. Let us take an example: An apple has a color, texture, size, shape, smell, and a taste of its own. Thanks to these characteristics, one can know whether such an object is an apple, lemon, balloon, or something else. The same is not the same for numbers. A group of seven things may have nothing in common with another group of seven objects other than that they are seven. Also, grasping the meaning of numbers, the difference between six and seven, for example, comes down to understanding something very abstract. Moreover, this is where the followers of numerology come into the picture.

In antiquity, it was common to lend a special meaning to numbers. Pythagoras, a Greek philosopher and mathematician who lived a century (BCE), taught that all things are numbers. He and his supporters held the whole universe as a model of proportion and harmony. Therefore, could it not be that all things obey mathematical laws? Since Pythagoras, numerical analyses have been used for predictions, dreams interpretation, and memorization. Greeks, Muslims, and Christians resorted to it.

In my case, I used the biblical meaning of those numbers as follows: the number 7 symbolizes *spiritual perfection*, something complete. In other words, fullness, divine perfection in spiritual things but also the relationship of the things of God with the earth.

The number 3 symbolizes the *divine fullness* and the perfection of the testimony. It is the divine figure—the number of the divine Trinity and the perfect testimony.

The symbolic number 2 means *precision*, witness, and communion. The two often appear in a legal context.

Principle 322: Spiritual Principle of Ideal Management

To construct the spiritual principle of ideal management, we will consider the number 3 for divine fullness, 2 for precision or communion, and 7 for what is complete (spiritual perfection). If we try to translate these figures by their meaning, we will have the following operation: 3 + 2 + 2 = 7 which equates to fullness + precision + communion = spiritual or complete perfection.

This means that there is a spiritual revelation or divine principle that we should know through this spiritual mathematical operation. This is what I call the ideal spiritual management principle. Management of what? We can group it into three broad categories of all God gives us: wealth, health, and satisfaction or happiness.

God always provides what is complete; it always gives everyone seven parts. Three of these seven parts belong to him in his spiritual management principle. We give him these three parts (divine fullness) through tithes, offerings, thanksgiving, etc. The four remaining parts must be shared or subject to communion with your neighbor with precision, two pieces for the neighbor and two for you according to the principle, "Love thy neighbor as you love yourself." Let us give an example: you receive a salary of 7,000 USD. The 3,000 USD should be used in God's work by first giving, inevitably, at least 700 USD of the tithe.

I say well, at least because by law, we offer a tenth of what we receive, but by grace, God gave us the best he had: his only son who gave himself as a ransom for our sins who took our sins on him for us to be justified. As a result, we should also show by grace and not by law. I am convinced that grace is superior to the law because it is simply an undeserved favor. This grace means that God gives the person what he requires of him. God cannot ask you what he did not give you. And according to his word in Psalm 24:1, everything belongs to him.

Of the 4,000 USD that remain, you should use half to support the poor, help others through all kinds of good deeds, and the other half for you. This is the ideal management that God wants us to apply and to get there. Other intermediate principles need to be understood and applied—to live the word of God. That is why it is clearly said that giving is more pleasurable than receiving. Giving is the only action that can tempt God and compel him to respond by abundance. The more you give, the more blessed you are. That is why even in this principle, the basis is to give and receive more. Three parts given to God and two to the neighbor will constitute the seed that God will multiply abundantly. You will be blessed above what you ask and even what you think. Hence, your descendants will inherit from your wealth.

Chapter 15

The Process Matters

The manufacturer assigns a modus operandi for every product and service. Every work must be operated in a specific method. If someone attempts to change the operating processes, they either will not work or work at a low-efficiency level. However, once someone learns the proper method for the process, he can operate them with a high degree of efficiency.

The same principle applies in all spheres of life. All things have a process. There is a correct way to operate that process. There are many ways we could choose to conduct our lives. There are processes in life that lead to a deep sense of fulfillment. There are also processes in life that can lead to a great sense of hurt, hollow existence, and hopelessness. It is up to us to decide which way we choose. God has placed a tiny part of his sovereignty on the shelf so that each of us might have freedom of choice. Just as everything has a process, so also God has a process.

The story of the prodigal son found in Luke 15:11–24 provides us with one of God's process-rejoicing methods. It consists of repentance, restoration, and rejoicing. For God, the end does not justify the means. God's work must be initiated by God and done at its time with the dedicated process and the intended results.

The ultimate example in demonstrating that the process matters is in the book of 2 Samuel 6:1–7. The story is about Uzzah's death punishment for what we might consider a good deed. However, the alleged good act violated God's process. No matter how innocently it was done, touching the ark violated God's law and was to result in death. Also, David used other men to collect the ark rather than allow the Levites to bring it to him. That was another violation of God's process. Thirdly, the ark should never have been put upon a cart, old or new. It was to be carried by Levites only upon their shoulders. The process each one uses to prepare his descendants matters. God's methods are irrevocable.

Section 7

Legacy

Chapter 16

Understanding Why We Do What We Do

One of the most challenging questions we have been asked is, "What do you do?" The typical response is, for example, I am the CEO of Feal enterprise. I am the security officer at Securicom. Ironically, nobody cares about what you do. They are interested in why you do what you do.

Some years back, I was hired by an organization. During the induction meetings, I was asked to introduce myself. Everyone expected me to disclose my name, carrier experience, and achievement. Instead, after saying my name, I added that I was born to inspire and ignite positive change in people's lives by bringing light to generational success. I elaborated that I joined the mission because I knew I could contribute to bringing about a new spirit to achieve more. Telling people why I joined the mission opened the mind of the director. She deployed me to the most sensitive and affected area where the office needed more improvement. Some of the high management members did not agree with the director as I was the newest staff member in the team. However, the decision was already made. After two years, the whole squad acknowledged that since the organization's opening, the two years were the most productive with a high-level team spirit.

The starting point of a sustainable legacy is the *why* which gives a clear sense and importance of what we want to leave after our death. This is not about qualifications but understanding what we can contribute to advance the future generations' mission, vision, and purpose.

The most important thing is to know the kind of fruit you can bring to feed the world. You are a seed God has produced, and according to Genesis 1:11, the Bible says,

> And God said, Let the earth bring forth grass, the herb yielding seed, and the fruit tree yielding fruit after his kind, whose origin is, upon the earth: and it was so.

Every source has a plant; holding a seed in your hand, you own a tree. I may say you are holding a forest in your hand because the tree in your hand yields fruits with seeds. If you knew what kind of seed you are, we would know what tree and forest you produce. The forest is essential to our life as it has what is needed to live. You are, therefore, important in our lives.

Nevertheless, to become the tree you already are and then the forest, you must go through and follow a process with no shortcut. Everyone was born to become a tree, and they must undergo a procedure to express their original identity. For example, all butterflies must undergo a complete metamorphosis process in four stages to grow into an adult: egg, larva, pupa, and adult. Each step has a different goal; for instance, caterpillars need to eat a lot, and adults need to reproduce. To become a butterfly, a caterpillar first digests itself. The process begins with a ravenous caterpillar hatching from an egg. The caterpillar stuffs itself with leaves, growing plumper and longer through a series of molts in which it sheds its skin. One day, the caterpillar stops eating, hangs upside down from a twig or leaf, and spins itself into a silky cocoon or molts into a shiny chrysalis. The caterpillar transforms its body within its protective casing eventually emerging as a butterfly. The caterpillar digests itself releasing enzymes to dissolve its tissues. However, certain groups of cells survive turning the soup into eyes, wings, antennae, and other adult structures.

As for the butterfly, you need to go through such transformations. The Scripture confirms this in the good news of John 12:24:

> Most assuredly, I say to you, unless a grain of
> wheat falls into the ground and dies, it remains
> alone; but if it dies, it produces much grain.

The process is straightforward. You must be planted in the background. A seed remains if it remains in the store and has no fruits or does not multiply. You should be willing to move out of your comfort zone. A planted seed needs nutrients from the soil and moisture to produce abundant fruits. Time is an essential factor depending on the kind of seed. Some seeds need more patience, perseverance, and faith than others.

According to the story of the Chinese bamboo tree, growing it requires nurturing—water, fertile soil, and sunshine. In its first year, there are no visible signs of activity. In the following three years, there is no growth above the ground. And finally, in the fifth year, change is visible. The story says the Chinese bamboo tree grows eighty feet in just six weeks! The way to produce our fruits also differs.

Bamboos are the fastest-growing plant on earth. A typical bamboo grows as much as ten centimeters a single day. The flowering of bamboo is an intriguing phenomenon because it is a unique and rare occurrence in the plant kingdom. Most bamboo flower once every 60 to 130 years. The long flowering intervals remain a mystery to many botanists. These slow-flowering species exhibit another strange behavior: they flower all at the same time, all over the world, irrespective of geographic location and climate as if they were derived from the same mother plant. Once a bamboo specie has reached its life expectancy, has flowered, and produced seeds, the plant dies, wiping out entire swaths of forests over several years.

Your fruit or gift is first hidden before it exposes itself. The time it takes to be seen depends on the kind of seed in you. It must also push through the soil and fight against obstacles to become visible on the surface. At that stage, the sun's rays are necessary to start the critical role of photosynthesis. To perform photosynthesis, plants need three things: carbon dioxide, water, and sunlight. Taking in water through the root hairs from the soil, carbon dioxide from the air, and light energy from the sun provide power for photosynthesis. Plants can perform photosynthesis to make glucose and oxygen. This means that you need external inputs and processes in your life to develop you and help you to become who you are. The soil, nutrient, water, and sun do not create the tree already existing in the seed. They are conducive conditions to activate what was already present. To become yourself and impact the world, even your descendants must be in a conducive and adequate environment.

You are a seed that bears fruits that your generations need to live better. As seeds are loaded, none is born empty. The fruits we need are your gift. I was born to inspire and ignite positive change in people's lives by bringing light to my generation for God's glory. People do not come to you but for your gift. The multiple processes you need to throw are only for the fruit. And that fruit is not yours. No tree has eaten his fruits. You exist to serve your generation. When you know your gift, people will find you, and then you will impact them. Knowing your gift is the key to generational success. The more you know who you are and what you do, the clearer we see what we expect from you. This provides a clear filter for decision-making and problem-solving in every area. It also helps you and everyone around you know which is the right advice for them to follow or not. What you do is supposed to be tangible proof of what you believe and who you are.

Chapter 17

Understanding Your Identity

The most beautiful lady in the world can only offer what she has. The disaster is to own a treasure and ignore that it is yours. Everyone needs to recognize and understand who he is and what he has. Then his descendants will inherit his riches. You need to believe consistently.

I was traveling from one city to another by plane. At boarding time, the commander asked to stop the process. At first, no reason was given. Half an hour later, an announcement came out: the flight was delayed for technical failure. Passengers were asked to wait until further notice. Four hours later, another call for boarding was shared. What intrigued me was not the delay of the flight and its consequences on the journey continuation but the way passengers were running to board the plane first. It takes an attitude of believing to rush on a plane with an announced technical problem just a couple of hours before. I wrote this story while on the same plane after two hours of flight.

How can we believe that a plane will safely take us to the destination but fail to believe in ourselves? Airplanes are built by humans that find it difficult to believe in themselves. The plane can make it, but you always complain that you can achieve nothing because you were born in a remote area. You say you are not from America, Europe, or a developed economy.

Don't you believe you are an original, wonderful, and fearful creature rather than a copy? You can leave a tremendous legacy to your generation in life, business, government, church, family, education, or any organization. But you will only transfer what you have. Everything starts by believing in yourself, your authority, your identity, your riches, and your manufacturer. You have been struggling with what people say about you, the names you are given, the success and results you are expected to achieve. It is time you understand that you are not what people want you to be. You are the one your Maker says you are. People see you today, but I would challenge you to see you after your death. What will the generations inherit from you? That is possible if you understand who you are and start living accordingly. Detect what enters you through your ears and eyes and start living what you are.

A young man named Jesus conversed with his disciples more than two thousand years ago. He asked them who people say he is. The disciples gave many names that had nothing to do with the person himself. Have you ever asked yourself whom people think you are? I know they have given a couple of names. That may be the reason you have a nickname. But I want to assure you that the true you will come from your inside. Whom do you believe you are? Do not wait for someone to tell you who you are. When people greet each other in my culture, they say hello. How are you doing? The answer is, "Things are not well. I am trying. It is good." I decide to say hello. I am doing well. How are you? The only person that can change your operating environment is yourself.

Know What You Are

Realize that each option has advantages and disadvantages. There is no right or wrong choice. There is a choice that one makes according to what he is. So being is more important than choosing. Indeed, it is necessary to work its character to be the one that one wants to be and make a good choice. To know who you are, you must know who you are not. This biblical passage tells us more:

> Here is the testimony of John, when the Jews
> sent priests and Levites from Jerusalem to ask

him: Who are you? He declared and did not deny him, he stated that he was not Christ. And they asked him: what then? Are you Elijah? And he said: I am not. Are you the Prophet? And he replied: No. Then they said: Who Are you? So that we could answer those who sent us. What do you think of yourself? He said I am the voice of the one who cries in the wilderness: smooth the way of the Lord, as Isaiah said, the prophet. (John 1:19–23)

This passage is self-explanatory. John was asked who he was to the extent that he saw himself as a particular person different from the others. They even tried to guide his answer by the ideas they had in mind. It is always like this. People always want to shape everything according to what they already know. But John knew who he was not, and it served as a defining area for others to know who he was. He said he was not Christ, Elijah, or the prophet.

But he said what he was: "I am the voice of the one who cries in the wilderness." Knowing what you are not will help you understand who you are and make choices based on what you are. For example, if you are a king and a priest, as the Bible calls those in Christ, you will not make the same choice as that of a thief. I am well aware that the right choice of a thief is to kill, destroy, and plunder because it is his character. But the right choice for a king is to be a good leader for his kingdom.

Look how Simon was informed of who Jesus was. It is straightforward to the question of Jesus. The disciples were saying what people thought according to what they wanted or their knowledge: John the Baptist, Elijah, Jeremiah, one of the prophets. But Simon, by divine revelation, found the correct answer. That means if you know Jesus, he will tell you precisely what you are. To understand what you are, you must first know who Jesus is. I know him as my personal Lord and Savior of my life. How about you? Eventually, you will make choices based on your real identity.

Chapter 18

Understanding the Operating Environment

Lions and other animals mark their territories. How about you? Animals know their abilities and capabilities. How about you? That is only possible if you know who you are. I remember I was in college when I took driving lessons. During the same period, my brother returned home after twenty-five years of exile in a European country. He was wealthy, intelligent, and respected. I had to shop for his special meals. One day, I took his car and bought some fruits and vegetables far from home. When I was back, he forbade me to drive his car anymore. I should buy mine. I was emotionally disappointed. However, the event challenged me to work hard until I purchased my vehicle. Ten years later, I succeeded in buying one. I was able to drive him and was emotionally satisfied.

Since then, I have understood that, irrespective of circumstances, I am blessed. What do I mean by that?

We operate in a blessed environment. To be blessed is to speak well of, cause to prosper, release the potential, beautify, or confer a benefit. The Scriptures say in Ephesians 1:3,"

> Blessed be the God and Father of our Lord Jesus Christ, who hath blessed us with all spiritual blessings in heavenly places in Christ.

Since God is acting in this verse, we can say that God has spoken good things about us or pronounced good things for our benefit. God has decreed for us good things beyond our ability to number as the Bible says in Ephesians 3:20,

> Now to him who can do immeasurably more than
> all we ask or imagine, according to his power that
> is at work within us.

God created us to accomplish something that must necessarily contribute to creating a good environment conducive to realizing His plan for his children on earth from generation to generation.

For example, God created Abraham to become the father of a chosen nation. Joseph was born to solve the famine problem for Egypt and its nation of Israel. Moses was not killed when he was born but preserved to liberate the children of God from the slavery of Egypt. Paul existed to preach the good news to the Gentiles. Because of him, we have the gospel, we are counted among the children of God, and are coheirs of Jesus and heirs of God. You are also born for a great purpose for your generation.

Two Are Better Than One

The generation needs you. Your fellow need you. Elisha needed Elijah to have the double portion of his anointing and perform the miracles he did. Elisha also needed Elijah for an effective ministry. Joshua needed the company of a great man of God, Moses, to lead the people of Israel into the promised land. Moses also needed Joshua as much as his right arm in all battles. David needed good company from Jonathan to escape the search for Saul and finally become the king of Israel who has a heart of God. Jonathan needed David to take a company with good people that have advantages that cannot all be listed here. Still, among other things, without pretending to be exhaustive, we can cite capacity building and career development or department in any area we serve. This is possible because a relationship with the successors reinforces the transitions, passing on power, or anointing. This only perpetuates the activity for the benefit of all.

A good company also helps to promote diversity. The latter is a source of intellectual wealth and an important factor in technical, numerical, financial, and material development. Have a company with good people, and God will multiply and bless you forever.

Two is better than one: Peter needed Jesus to become the leader who exhorted others. Timothy needed Paul to continue the work of God that he had begun in the nations. You also need someone to become what God has prepared for you and his people through your work.

Jonathan needed David to take care of his orphan son after the death of the entire family of King Saul. Peter needed Jesus to become the leader who exhorted others. Also, Timothy needed Paul to continue the work of God that he had begun in the nations. But Paul also needed Timothy and Titus to strengthen and build the churches he had opened. You also need someone to become what God has prepared for you and his people through your work. Do not forget that someone also needs you, so release your potential.

Stay close to me. You have great importance in my life. I am also willing to stay by your side. The Bible tells us this:

> But to each, the manifestation of the Spirit is given for common utility. (1 Corinthians 12:7)

This means that everyone has received from God an invaluable treasure that makes him valuable to others. Each of us has a divine brand; we all complement each other. This usefulness in diversity comes from the creativity of God and makes each one incomparable and original.

There is no filthy trade but dirty people. When I finished college, our country was going through an unprecedented crisis. So it was difficult to get a job for one reason: my family had to live. My wife also graduated in the same conditions. After a concerted decision, we started a small business selling palm oil. Our initial capital was five liters of palm oil. Two college graduates with a capital of five liters of palm oil! There is something to be ashamed of. The Bible says in Luke 16:10–12,

> He who is faithful in the minor things is also in the great, and the one who is unfair in the little things is also in the great. Who will entrust you with the true ones if you have not been faithful in the unjust wealth? And if you have not been faithful in what is to others, who will give you what is yours?

This small business could help us buy a light daily meal. We added interest to the capital and moved from five liters to twenty liters and then moved to the status of wholesalers. We start from the minimum to the maximum: little by little, the bird nests. What is valid for the bird is also true for a man. What is true for an elephant is also for an ant. Whatever small or big you do, this is about your generation and your offspring.

We are created to impact the world and leave a legacy for the next generation. We must be diligent. As the Scripture says in the book of Proverbs 21:5,

> The projects of the diligent man lead only to abundance, but he who acts with haste only arrives at the scarcity.

Only then will our fruitfulness be helpful. Blessings come not from the abundance of sleep but from diligence and courage. A singer said, "If the first time you fail, try a second time. If the thirteenth time you fail, try a fourteenth time." The singer stopped at thirteen, but I would say that we must continue until the day of Christ. Edison has tried one thousand times; today, we have electric tubes and press a switch to have light. However, it took him a crazy effort to succeed. Why not you and me?

You Are the Product of Your Choices

These children grew up. Esau became a skillful hunter, a man of the fields, But Jacob was a quiet man who remained under the tents. (Genesis 25:27)

When making your choice, think about your children and generation. You can be born under identical conditions, eat the same food or meal, attend the same school and church, occupy the same positions, and have the same salary. The difference will always be determined by the choice of each one. Each one is therefore called to make choices every day or at any moment. We choose what we eat, where to live, friends, church, country, etc. Choosing is one thing. Making a good choice is another. The Bible says,

Teach me common sense and intelligence because
I believe in your commandments. (Psalm 119:66)

Chapter 19

A Good Company

Make no mistake: bad companies corrupt good morals.

—1 Corinthians 15:33

The bad companies are people who whisper, complain about their fate, walk according to their lusts, have haughty words, and admire people because of interest. Such people cause divisions in the assemblies; they are often unhappy with their situation and go as far as to discourage believers in their Christian march by provoking divisions. Hence, when faced with individuals who fail to trust the Lord God, caution must be exercised.

What corrupts good morals is not only the habitual and intimate society of people of evil morals, but it is still the mere sight, the only hearing, the only contact of what is wrong. It is not necessary to live or only to have frequentations with the wicked; all you must do is look, reach your ear, or move your hand over the works.

It is up to us to pay attention to our frequentations. To be concerned with those who seem harmless because they are normal relationships. I think of the neighborhood relations with which we must be on good terms while being prepared to do them good every time the opportunity is given to us as faithful witnesses of Jesus Christ. Avoid at all costs following the villain and accompanying him in his activities! To be his companion of works, to be an accomplice who will benefit from the "fraternal" sharing of the proceeds of the evil deeds committed together. Also, avoid performing the same works as the villain without walking by his side.

I remember Jesus telling his disciples that he was going to his father's house. Everyone was desperate, but he encouraged them by reassuring them that he left for their sake. A separation for people on good terms should only be done for an interest superior to both parties.

A good company strengthens or increases the performance of partners. What one cannot achieve can be done with the assistance of his companion if someone manages to do a new action. It becomes an additional strength or asset. Each has a different potential, but the potential increases, the performance increases, the efficiency increases, and the result increases accordingly. And the world has so much need for results; One of the solutions is to have a good company. What a source of blessings!

Good company strengthens and creates a line of good leaders in all areas of life where this principle is applied. When I was pursuing my studies at the University of Burundi, a friend had a scholarship abroad only because he was named after someone who had a good relationship with people in Burundi. My colleague was not a member of this noble family, but the people who studied the files wanted to reward a lineage or kinship of the right person. God gives in abundance! Burundi has a high-level leader because of a person who has applied the principle of having a good company. The country is blessed through one person, without mentioning the families. If the people to whom you and I applied this principle, the families, the churches, the organizations, and the countries could benefit from this divine blessing.

A company with good people has advantages that cannot be listed here. Still, among other things, without pretending to be exhaustive, we can cite capacity building and career development or ministry in any area we serve. This is possible because a personal relationship with the successors reinforces the transitions or passing on of power or anointing. This only perpetuates the business activity for the benefit of all.

A good company also helps to promote diversity. The latter is a source of intellectual and spiritual wealth and an essential factor in technical, numerical, financial, and material development. Have company with good people, and God will multiply and bless you forever.

Chapter 20

Keep the Promise

Know how to respect, and love what is good and sweet for you. Have the right to be demanding about their well-being. Respect their choices and do not, especially, regret and an attitude to encourage. A friend once told me that despair is a rendezvous for success. The main thing is to stay calm and gentle with a positive attitude even under challenging conditions.

In any case, God has confidence in you and can never allow a situation that is beyond your control to happen to you. If, in some cases, it becomes difficult to resist, God is always there to intervene (1 Corinthians 10:13). In the end, we must stop at all costs to believe that a person must suffer to advance and to think that you have no right to be happy. It all comes down to staying fit and knowing each other well.

The Best Choice

There is no salvation in any other, for there is no other name under heaven which has been given among men, by which we must be saved. (Acts 4:12)

> Jesus said to him: I am the way, the truth, and the
> life. No one comes to the father but me. (John
> 14:6)

Every day, we make thousands of choices. Some choices have more impact on our lives than others. Others require deep reflection while others might even demand the input of others. Making Jesus the Lord of your life is the best choice you could ever make! However, once you have chosen it, you can make choices to support this noble choice daily. For example, are you choosing to serve the Lord with your attitude? Have you decided to serve the Lord with your finances? Have you chosen to serve the Lord by what you say? What are you watching on TV? What are you listening to?

Today, I encourage you to examine your thoughts and actions. Choose this day to serve him in all areas of your life. As you submit your ways, he promises to lead your steps. Remember, he has for you good things in reserve for the future. He promises to give you the means to live a life of victory if you choose it daily.

Forgive

> Jesus said unto him: I do not tell you up to seven
> times, but up to seven times seven times. (Mat
> 18:22)

Forgiveness is tough, but forgiveness is one of the essential conditions for good company. For our Lord Jesus, everyone must be prepared to forgive the same person every two minutes. It is crucial to have a good choice, especially a good friend.

Thank God for your choice.

> I am the vine; you are the branches. The one who
> abides in me and in whom I remain bears a great
> deal of fruit, for you can do nothing without me.
> (John 15:5)

Making a good choice requires divine intervention. Jesus says that no one can do anything good without him. Especially since we are fallible humans, everyone can commit a fault or a mistake. So you do not have to lose your self-confidence because you have not made a good choice for one or two. The singer said, "If the first time you do not succeed, you have to try a second time."

About the Author

Dr. Ferdinand Nduwindavyi holds MA in leadership and management from Anglia Ruskin University in the UK and a doctorate in business administration—global leadership from California Intercontinental University in the USA. He has served with the United Nations System for twenty-five years as a human rights officer.

He's an overseer of the Church on the Rock Burundi for more than thirteen years; he is an inspirational speaker on leadership and management at several platforms including with Global Leadership Summit.

He is currently the president of Victory Bible College, Bujumbura, Burundi. He is the author of "Conseils de Vie" and multiple other pamphlets on different subjects.

www.ingramcontent.com/pod-product-compliance
Lightning Source LLC
Chambersburg PA
CBHW020257180726
47994CB00027B/932